STUDIES IN COMPARATIVE POLITICS

The purpose of the collection 'Studies in Comparative Politics' is to provide the students of politics with a series of up-to-date, short, and accessible surveys of the progress of the discipline, its changing theoretical approaches and its methodological reappraisals.

The format of the individual volumes is understandably similar. All authors examine the subject by way of a critical survey of the literature on the respective subject, thus providing the reader with an up-to-date *bibliographie raisonnée* (either separate or contained in the text). Each author then proposes his own views on the future orientation. The style tries to bridge the often lamented gap between the highly specialised language of modern political science and the general reader. It is hoped that the entire collection will be of help to the students who try to acquaint themselves with the scholarly perspectives of contemporary politics.

S. E. Finer
Ghiţa Ionescu

Already published

LESLIE J. MACFARLANE: Political Disobedience
ROGER WILLIAMS: Politics and Technology
WILLIAM WALLACE: Foreign Policy and the Political Process
W. J. M. MACKENZIE: The Study of Political Science Today
GHIŢA IONESCU: Comparative Communist Politics

Forthcoming titles

C. H. DODD: Political Development
BERNARD CRICK: Elementary Types of Government
LESLIE WOLF-PHILLIPS: Comparative Constitutions
A. H. BROWN: Soviet Politics and Political Science
DENNIS KAVANAGH: Political Culture
S. E. FINER: The Study of Interest Groups
GEOFFREY K. ROBERTS: What is Comparative Politics?

STUDIES IN COMPARATIVE POLITICS
published in association with
GOVERNMENT AND OPPOSITION

a quarterly journal of comparative politics, published by Government and Opposition Ltd., London School of Economics and Political Science, Houghton Street, London, W.C.2.

Comparative Communist Politics

GHIŢA IONESCU

Professor of Government, University of Manchester

Macmillan

First published 1972 by
THE MACMILLAN PRESS LTD
London and Basingstoke
Associated companies in New York Toronto
Dublin Melbourne Johannesburg and Madras

SBN 333 13301 3

Printed in Great Britain by
THE ANCHOR PRESS LTD
Tiptree, Essex

CONTENTS

1. A RECAPITULATION

This survey will attempt to assess the present state of that sub-group, or offshoot, of the discipline of comparative politics* which deals with communist politics and sees them as part of the contemporary political world. Yet the reader should note from the beginning that the operative word in the expression is *politics*. This approach distinguishes, to a certain degree, this work from previous surveys appearing under the more general name of either 'comparative communism' or 'comparative communist studies'. There will be frequent references in these pages to the question whether, generally speaking, the entire discipline of comparative politics is not now going through a crisis of reassessment.

The International Political Science Association Round Table held at Turin in September 1969 on this very subject emphasised the need for a critical reconsideration, for an attempt to find new methodological means leading out of the cul-de-sac in which the discipline has wandered. The tone was set by Gabriel Almond, who has done more than anyone else to present comparative politics as a self-contained, modern discipline :

> A mood of disillusionment appears to be sweeping the field of comparative politics and political development. This comes after almost two decades of rather impressive accomplishment, both from a qualitative and quantitative point of view. . . . [It is] the intractability of human affairs, the disorderliness and unpredictability of the processes of change that are the principal causes of the intensity of our current unrest. We are not the first generation of political theorists to discover that the problem of explanation in social and political affairs is an extremely

---

* See, in this series, Geoffrey Roberts, *What is Comparative Politics?* (forthcoming).

difficult one, that the problem of prediction comes close to being insoluble. . . .[1]

The basic report at the Turin conference was presented by Giovanni Sartori. It has since been published as Sartori's important study 'Concept Misformation in Comparative Politics'.[2] Having described the present plight of political science 'as the oscillation between the extreme, on the one hand, of unconscious and, on the other, of overconscious thinking with a wide gap between them which is concealed by the growing sophistication of statistical and research technique', Sartori diagnoses the difficulties of present political science as 'methodological unawareness'. And he stresses that 'the study of comparative politics is particularly vulnerable to, and illustrative of, this infelicitous state of affairs'. He believes that the present confusion created in the study of politics by the excessive use of quantification is due to the fact that it was forgotten that 'concept formulation stands prior to quantification'. The lower the discriminating conceptual power, the more the facts are misgathered, i.e. the greater the misinformation – and vice versa. Sartori sees the obvious solution in employing a correct 'ladder of abstraction' which should observe three levels of abstraction and conceptualisation – of which more will be said later in this survey. But only by applying severely the rules of logic can the present 'comparative fallacies', 'comparative stretching' and 'conceptual misformation' be stopped. The discipline will continue to 'swim in a sea of empirical and theoretical messiness'.

It is therefore not surprising that such views should be echoed with reference to the sub-discipline of comparative communist politics, which suffers even more from the present imprecision. The following is a typical example of the expression of disappointment and bewilderment produced by the introduction of comparative 'stretching' and 'fallacies' in the field of communist studies :

> Students of Communist systems have long attempted to devise a general model that would identify the central or characteristic elements of a Communist system and provide a clear basis for distinguishing Communist from other types of politics. . . . It is characteristic of both the comparative and Communist

8

fields that over the past few years the number and particularity of such models have been increasing rather than decreasing. This suggests that as our knowledge of the workings of various types of political systems increases and becomes more detailed, it becomes more and more difficult to devise general models that can comprehend all the major dimensions of modern political life. . . . In this way, the very exercise of systematic model-building can obstruct comparative empirical research.

This citation comes from *Communist Studies and the Social Sciences*, a symposium edited by Frederic J. Fleron Jr.[3] This useful collection of essays, very relevant to this subject, brings together the most interesting papers written over the last ten years in the United States, where studies of both comparative politics and comparative communism have flourished.

This survey will try to offer a brief summary in a very limited space of the different trends and phases which have emerged in the field of comparative communist politics in what must be considered a most fruitful decade. Indeed, it was only as recently as 1959 that Philip Mosely, one of the principal initiators of systematic communist studies in the U.S.A., declared that 'An important task which has hardly been tackled at all is the comparative study of Communist systems'. Looked at in retrospect, the work achieved since then is so vast and so varied, that its exaggerations, deviations and vagaries can still be considered as, to use a Leninist expression, 'infantile diseases'.

THE NON-COMPARATIVE METHOD

This rapid progress is even more impressive if one remembers that at the beginning, the effort to bring together communist studies into some general comparative framework had to overcome the assumption, widely entertained for at least two different reasons, that studies of communism were essentially non-comparative. This led to a professional deformation, a kind of esotericism.

One reason for this esotericism was the fact that during the first period of research, studies of communist politics were invariably monographs on separate countries, states and periods. The esotericism of the approach was due not to broad ideological considerations but, on the contrary, to the exclusive concen-

9

tration of specialists on their subject matter. The scarcity of sources and contacts with the communist countries, at least until the mid-fifties, rendered it inevitable that the only authors and researchers able to study them were those who knew the languages concerned and were willing to do their own deductive research from the scant first-hand sources available or obtainable in the West. This is how 'sovietology' as a discipline, and historical analyses of the U.S.S.R., appeared. The academic students of the U.S.S.R. alone (Philip Mosely and Merle Fainsod in the U.S.A., Leonard Schapiro in Britain, Boris Meissner and Klaus Mehnert in Germany) were then followed by the students of Czechoslovakia, Poland, Hungary, Romania, Bulgaria, East Germany and, last but not least, China. (Another echelon of sovietology was formed by the principal newspapers' commentators on communist affairs: Edward Crankshaw, Victor Zorza, Michel Tatu, Harry Schwartz. Their spheres of analysis and forecasting were narrower than those of the Kremlinologists – Boris Meissner, Richard Loewenthal and, to a certain degree, Brzezinski – who distilled the general political and social analysis into actual predictions of the changes in the constellation of the leadership.)

The other, diametrically opposed, reason is to be found in the exclusive attitude of Marxist-Leninists towards their own theory and praxis. It was Lenin himself who imposed on communists a kind of *noli me tangere* of ideological purity. He believed that those who had accepted the dialectical materialist *Weltanschauung* should be completely immersed in its 'consciousness'. As dialectical materialism is, for Marxist-Leninists, both a new science and a new 'consciousness', which broke once and forever with the old bourgeois values and established its own tenets, no other method or system of global interpretation or of analytical projection could be reconciled with it. Besides, in the sphere of comparative politics the gap is all the more difficult to bridge in so far as all social studies are, from the Marxist-Leninist point of view, only one facet of global historical materialism. Comparative *political* studies are, in this perspective, exercises of measurement of dialectical progress made by contemporary societies from the pre-revolutionary stage to the socialist form and finally to the form of societies no longer political. Thus a historical-materialist comparative typology of contemporary states can be obtained by dividing all states first into capitalist or non-capitalist, and the latter into national democracies, people's democracies, socialist republics – and finally the as yet unattained phase of communist *society*, which is therefore no longer a *state*. This typology could be *translated* into plain language (and indeed it offers some similarity with the theories of economic development), but in the view of Marxist-Leninist ideologists it should not be brought back to or made to correspond with what they considered to be the obselete positions of alleged objectivity. To embrace by means of allegedly 'comparative' methods, in one global vision, the world of the past together with the world of the future would be, from a militant vantage-point, tantamount to ideological treason.

This belief, that communist politics form a non-comparable category of their own, has also influenced Western authors of independent political complexion. Such scholars accepted as a premise of their investigation that communist political and ideological matters have to be observed and studied only within their own terms of reference. Some, like the historian E. H. Carr, although himself remaining on the pre-Leninist, non-historical-materialist side of 'objectivity', assumed, however, that a kind of methodological dichotomy had once and forever been effected. Thus :

A history of Soviet Russia written by an Englishman who has neither a Marxist nor a Russian background may seem a particularly hazardous enterprise. No sensible person will be tempted to measure the Russia of Lenin, Trotsky and Stalin by any yardstick borrowed from the Britain of MacDonald, Baldwin and Churchill or the America of Wilson, Hoover and Franklin Roosevelt.[4]

Yet, in spite of this self-imposed handicap, Carr detected, with the sound instinct of a political historian, the importance of the re-birth in Russia of the supreme, and universally comparable, political institution, namely the state. He described this process with great accuracy, and with greater emphasis than many other historians and political scientists have done since. He rightly interpreted it as the turning-point away from the deeper meaning of the revolution and against its specific institution, the

11

soviets, which the state easily destroyed in its functional march to arch-centralism.

The same cannot be said of the biographer Isaac Deutscher who, for instance, in spite of calling his *Stalin* 'a political biography', remained throughout this work a dialectical visionary with characteristic *apolitical* millenarianism. Thus, although he clearly perceived Lenin's and, later, Stalin's Jacobinism, he saw it only in terms of the comparison between the French and the Russian revolutions. He did not draw the political conclusions of the recurrence in both revolutions of the Jacobin *political institutions* : the nation-state, the centralistic administration and the dictatorial party. Unlike Carr, and indeed unlike Lenin, Deutscher in his 'political' biography of Stalin deliberately refused to analyse the relations between the 'state' and the 'revolution' which involve the direct *political* approach to the question. His approach remained historical and millenarian and is best defined by the title of one of his last works, *The Unfinished Revolution*, and especially in another of his last works, this time on a plainly political subject : 'The Roots of Bureaucracy'. Here we see Deutscher fully aware of the fact that 'the old cleavage between the men of property and the property-less masses gives place to another division, different in character but no less noxious and corrosive : the division between the rulers and the ruled, and that far from withering away the state reaches its apotheosis'.[5] But instead of joining in an objective examination of this perennial and general *political* truth, Deutscher preferred to defer judgement for teleological reasons. He concluded his incipient analysis by saying abruptly that when the perfect utopian, classless, society should, one day, be established, 'it will be seen that if bureaucracies were a faint prelude to class society, bureaucracy will mark the fierce ferocious epilogue to class society, no more than an epilogue'.[6]

It is this millenarian approach of the historical-materialist political students which, in principle, compels them to exclude communist revolutions and their aftermaths from the general study of politics. This kind of study, in their view, applies only to class and politics in pre-revolutionary societies. But the new post-revolutionary societies should be described only in their own terms.

The elusiveness of such terms and of the frontiers between such categories as state, dictatorship of the proletariat, soviet-state, commune-state or withering-away state, and generally speaking between the allegedly disappearing political institutions and the allegedly omnipotent social organisations, combined with the difficulty of using scholarly reliable first-hand data, have had a negative effect also on Western political scientists and theorists. As a whole they have preferred to deal directly as little as possible with these involved phenomena. They have preferred to leave this area of study to the 'sovietologists' and/or the sociologists whose looser and more easily adjustable methods of study could find other paths through the revolutionary maze; or they have adopted only broad and normative comparable models.

THE TOTALITARIAN MODEL

One such broad comparative method by which all forms of the modern state could be embraced in one perspective was obtained by dividing them into totalitarian on the one hand and, on the other hand, democratic, liberal, free, representative, Western or pluralistic-constitutional states. The variety of definitions used in this approach to the non-totalitarian state reflects the extent to which they were comparatively defined *ex adverso* by all being pitted against one totalitarian model.

The model, subsuming the total control of the total society by the total means and for the total purposes of the state, originated probably with G. H. Sabine (1929) and Franz Neumann (1940) who introduced, before the Second World War, the quasi-metaphorical expression used by Italian fascists into academic language. But immediately after the Second World War a spate of impressive works by Karl Popper,[7] Hannah Arendt[8] and, later, J. Talmon[9] among others kindled the popular imagination with this concept. The initial analysis by Carl J. Friedrich and especially his *Totalitarian Dictatorship and Autocracy*, written together with K. Brzezinski,[10] provided the first systematic exposition in terms of political science of this comparative method. By proposing six basic features – an official ideology, a single mass party led typically by one man, a terroristic police, a communications monopoly, a weapons monopoly, and a centrally directed economy – Friedrich and Brzezinski provided the means of identification of the totalitarian state.

13

Although the features were ultimately relevant only to Nazi Germany and Stalinist Russia, they extrapolated them, with mixed fortunes, so as to make them fit all the other communist states and many of the nationalist dictatorships. Their definition was accepted by most schools of thought or textbooks of comparative politics (Almond, Roy C. Macridis, Raymond Aron, S. E. Finer and Jean Blondel among others) and by students of the Soviet Union (Leonard Schapiro, Merle Fainsod, Alex Inkeles, Barrington Moore among others), and still serves as the most widely accepted comparative criterion. The totalitarian – democratic dichotomy has been, and is, one of the few modern comparative approaches which has been of use both to scholars and to the public at large.

From the point of view of political theory and science, another advantage of the totalitarian concept lay in the fact that it concentrated on the effect that different institutions can have on societies. It is perhaps difficult, however, to compare from such a vantage-point the differences between the effects of the totalitarian Stalinist system and the pluralistic-constitutional system respectively on Russian society and on, say, American society between the two world wars. The formidable differences in background – levels of economic development, political culture, systems of communications, etc. – make the comparison circumstantial or anachronistic. But the effect of a given political system and of its institutions on societies can be highlighted in an adequate comparative manner in, for instance, the study of the German and the Russian societies of, say, 1929 and 1939; that is, before and after the acute period when the full totalitarian institutions had been set up. A safe comparison can be established between their respective effects. In this sense it might also be said that during the Stalinist period, for instance, the totalitarian model did provide an intra-area comparative yardstick as it served to measure the degree to which the then 'satellite' states succeeded or failed to reproduce the compulsory blueprint or indeed 'model' of the U.S.S.R. But the method, of course, became useless, indeed counter-productive, once the new Yugoslav, Polish and Chinese ideologies and approaches were put forward by their founders as distinct from, and opposed to, those of the U.S.S.R.

Of the major criticisms raised against totalitarianism as a comparative concept, the first is directly related precisely with the institutional approach. It was pointed out, on the one hand, that by concentrating on institutions the analysis missed the organic view of the revolutionary society, its true contents. Of this more will be said in the next section of this survey. But it was also pointed out that the totalitarian analysis, concentrating as it does on the effects of the use of political power on society, failed to locate that power. The theory that it was one tyrant who possessed all power, Hitler, Stalin, Mussolini, Mao or Franco, was criticised for obvious over-simplification. It did not fit the modern and elaborate system of contemporary tyrannies and would therefore be hard to distinguish from all forms of tyrannies known in history (indeed schools of thought developed which linked all Oriental despotisms together).

In the Friedrich–Brzezinski analysis, where the man was linked with the party, i.e. 'a single party typically headed by one man', all the other five features of totalitarianism pointed to the party as the main institution in totalitarianism. The same view was taken also by Merle Fainsod[11] in the U.S. who discarded, presumably as 'constitutional myths', the representative institutions of the U.S.S.R. and especially the soviets themselves and concentrated exclusively on the party; and by Leonard Schapiro in Britain, who even theorised this view[12] by propounding that totalitarianism is so arbitrary and, presumably, so *illegal* that it cannot even produce a *state* but only amorphous autocratic 'rule'. Concentration on the party has been, as will be shown later, criticised for producing a view of the political system of the communist state which (*a*) ignored or denied the reality of other political institutions with their own functional impact and with their intra-institutional conflicts; (*b*) did not take account of the intermittent nature of the power of the party: its eclipses and its rivalry with and replacement by other apparats like, above all, the political police; (*c*) came too close to the exaltation of the role of the communist parties made by themselves; and (*d*) overlooked the visible impact of the evolution of industrial societies, with the consequent development of pluralisation, on the allegedly monolithic states. An article by Karl Deutsch published in 1954 on 'Cracks in the Monolithic Possibilities and Patterns of Disintegration in Totalitarian Systems' was the earliest and remains one of the most cogent formulations of this critical line of thinking.

The second major criticism derived from the contention that the concept of 'totalitarianism' had proved much more appropriate for the comparison of the two rival contemporary dictatorial powers: Nazi Germany and Stalinist Russia. But after the collapse of the former, the de-Stalinisation of the latter and the emergence after the Second World War of so many other presumably 'totalitarian' (quasi-communist or quasi-fascist) states with different situations and backgrounds, the concept became too undiscriminating. Tito's Yugoslavia or Salazar's Portugal could not be described as identical with Stalin's Russia or Hitler's Germany. On the other hand, constantly to make use of qualifications and degrees in order to give flexibility to such an all-embracing concept could not but go against its essence. Like 'total', from which it derives, totalitarian cannot be graded. The recent attempts to establish classes and categories of totalitarianism not only failed, they also dissolved the notion.

Thus the efforts undertaken, especially since the fifties, to find new scientific methods for comparing the communist states with each other, and for comparing them and other non-communist categories of contemporary states, have also arisen because the concept of totalitarianism shrank so much and was less and less adapted to the diversity of situations and the variety of specimens in the continuum of dictatorial or authoritarian states in existence after the Second World War.

THE EXHORTATION

Following Mosely's appeal in 1959, sociologists and political scientists tried afresh to find new, comparative, methods for communist studies. It was actually a political scientist specialising in communist studies, H. Gordon Skilling, who was the first to raise the question in a study dedicated to this problem.[13] Robert C. Tucker (1967);[14] Paul Shoup (1968),[15] Frederic Fleron,[16] Jan Triska and R. Barrell (1968),[17] Chalmers Johnson (1969),[18] and, also, the author of this survey,[19] have all studied the same question in general terms, each in his own way. One of these ways, represented principally by Alfred G. Meyer (1967),[20] was to raise the question on the more specific issue of the need to replace the totalitarian model by new, more comprehensive and more value-free comparative approaches. As could be expected, Carl J. Friedrich and K. Brzezinski joined in the debate. But in the exercise they parted company, each producing new ideas on how to introduce greater flexibility into the definitions of totalitarianism.

All these studies and articles had in common a distinct exhortatory purpose and were more critical of the past than constructive for the future. This, of course, is a common characteristic of studies concerned with the methodology of disciplines, and especially in the field of social sciences. In some cases the, as it were, methodological preface is followed and illustrated by the work which is produced according to the new method. Apart from being a contribution to the subject matter, the work is also a proof of the originality of the method employed. But most methodological works only explain how the work should be done, according to new methods; they criticise the methods of the past but contribute very little to the substance. By the very fact that they are preparatory, they stop before the work is done only to advise how it should be done.

Comparative politics, in general, and comparative communist politics especially have not progressed much beyond the stage of methodological exhortation. Although the systemic approaches have generated many and very important studies, the largest part of political studies published nowadays, even in America but especially in Europe, does not acknowledge, or acknowledges only in part, the principles and methods of systemic comparative politics, or use their approaches and terminology. No school of comparative politics, and even less of comparative communism, has succeeded yet in uniting behind one method and one set of principles even those students who would accept the premise of the necessity of an organised comparative method.

Although the first exhortations (manifestos by individual authors, conferences and seminars called for the purpose of devising the consensual methods, or collective symposia or anthologies of articles) were issued a decade ago, studies of comparative politics, and communist studies in particular, are still in need of unification. Even today further conferences are called, and critical recapitulations are undertaken.

A simple, indeed probably over-simplified, view of the progress made up to now in comparative communist studies could be obtained by examining how the new methods of comparative politics have been applied to this sub-field. In order to do so it is perhaps useful to divide these methods into, first, the empirical approaches, and, second, the conceptual or, rather, reconceptualising approaches based on systems, models or frameworks of comparative political analysis.

Then, it will also be of help to apply to the sub-discipline of comparative communist politics Sartori's 'ladder of abstraction'[21] which is probably the clearest and fairest way of summing up the logical possibilities of comparative exercises:

Levels of abstraction	Major comparative scope and purpose	Logical and empirical properties of concept
High-level categories Universal conceptualisation	Cross-area comparisons among heterogeneous contexts (global theory)	Maximal extension Minimal intension Definition by negation
Medium-level categories General conceptualisation and taxonomies	Intra-area comparisons among relatively homogeneous contexts (middle-range theory)	Balance of denotation with connotation. Definition by analysis, i.e. per genus et differentiam
Low-level categories Configurative conceptualisation	Country by country analysis (narrow-gauge theory)	Maximal intension Minimal extension Contextual definition

A. THE EMPIRICAL APPROACHES

THE USES AND ABUSES OF QUANTIFICATION

By obtaining, collecting and quantifying the empirical observations (statistical data, interviews, etc.) the modern researchers offer to a discipline which was essentially historical and institutional new foundations of 'scientific' assessment and experimentation. This has led, and is leading, to the formation of the data-banks of social sciences, which are the bases of their new methodologies.

But the availability of data is precisely one of the greatest

18

divides between studies of comparative politics, in general, and the hoped-for extension of these studies to the special sector of comparative communist politics. Whereas in the non-communist states the data-banks and consortia grow continuously to unforeseen dimensions, in communist studies very little progress has been made, and then only in some communist states. Institutes of Social Research, and even of Public Opinion, have been set up in Yugoslavia, Poland, Hungary and Czechoslovakia,[22] and the Statistical Institutes of most of the communist states have undertaken presumably complete, detailed, and reliable censuses. But the data thus obtained are available only in some states and not in others. This renders both cross-area and intra-area comparative research very difficult. Moreover, even these data are not always, and never completely, available to Western students. To be sure, there is some ground for hoping that in the future things will improve. The trend in most of these states is towards modernisation of empirical research and the increase of collaboration with Western research centres, professional associations of social science and individual universtities. But until then most attempts made by Western social scientists to apply the methods of empirical research to communist states, based as they are on such incomplete and unreliable data as can be obtained today in most of them, are necessarily doomed to failure. Moreover they are, in such conditions, counter-productive, since they can lead to unwarranted or misleading conclusions.

A scholarly and painstaking work which was rewarded by a justified *succès d'estime* in the U.S.A. will be taken here as one example of the kind of study that might ultimately be counter-productive. If it is submitted here to a more detailed critical scrutiny it is only because it is representative of most of the 'contents-quantifying' research on official communist data.

The study is called *Soviet Elite Attitudes since Stalin* by Milton C. Lodge.[23] It is meant to be a comparative analysis of five Soviet élites – the full-time party functionaries (the 'apparat' élite and four 'specialist' élites : the 'economic administrators', the 'military', the 'literary intelligentsia' and the 'legal profession'. The object of the study is described thus : 'By content-analysing representative periodicals for each élite, data are collected on élite attitudes towards the Soviet political system'. This originally

19

value-free purpose is afterwards described more normatively by the statement that 'the overall goal is to determine the extent to which the apparat élite dominate the political process'; it acknowledges its intellectual links with previously established hypotheses 'derived in part from Brzezinski and Huntington's *Political Power: U.S.A./U.S.S.R.*', and more precisely with the hypothesis 'that in the post-Stalin period . . . the Party apparat, while still dominant in the political arena, is being forced to tolerate greater specialist élite participation in the political process'.

The double range of questions to be asked were:

A. How, when, why do the specialist élites differ from the Party apparat élite? Do the specialist élites share a set of beliefs and values which distinguish them from the full-time Party functionary? In sum, do the élites manifest the attitudinal make-up of the analytically distinct groups? B. Do the specialist élites perceive themselves as attitudinal participants in the Soviet political process? Do they *aspire* to a co-participant role with the *apparatchiki*? Are the specialist élites developing a set of participatory attitudes which tends to undermine the dominance of the Party apparat in policy-making and implementation?

The logic of the analysis proposed for this purpose is explained as follows:

Western analyses of Soviet politics must, *of necessity,* rely heavily on published sources. . . . Soviet spokesmen grudgingly acknowledge, and Western analyses have demonstrated, that specialist journals are vehicles for the *limited* articulation of élite attitudes. . . . The overwhelming majority of sampled articles are *achievement-oriented*. . . . Within this orientation authors are predominantly *concerned with specifics*. . . .

Yet, in spite of these formidable limitations it was still proposed to content-quantify articles published in Soviet journals, thus:

For each élite representative periodicals were selected for content analysis [two for the party apparat, three for the economic élite, one for the military, two for the legal profession and three for the literary élite]. . . . To satisfy the definitional

20

requirement of objectivity in content analysis, systematic samples procedures are required.

1. The unit of analysis is the article. Articles in the sample were chosen from the periodicals on the basis of a quota sample. . . .
2. The unit of enumeration, what is being coded and counted, is the major theme of a paragraph.
3. The size of the sample is equal for each élite each year, 600 paragraphs per élite for each of the eight sampled years – 1952, 1953, 1955, 1957, 1959, 1961, 1963, and 1965 – a yearly sample of 3000 paragraphs (600 paragraphs – 5 élites) for a total study sample of 24,000 paragraphs (3000 paragraphs per year × 8 years). [*our italics*]

A more detailed description of the methodology is given, for instance, in the working-out of *group self-consciousness:*

Group self-consciousness and ascribed group status are measured by a special word count category in which all references in the sampled articles which refer to one of the élites by means of a representative *collective noun* are tallied. . . . By coding all representative plural references (excluding all references to specific people and institutions) the collective noun connotes a perception of group status on the perceived élite by the perceiver.

The conclusions drawn on the basis of the extremely complicated operation of quantification thus proposed are that: 'In sum the Soviet political system is competitive. . . . Party specialist élite interdependence, not apparat-élite dominance, characterised Party relations'. This is further generalised in the final and dramatic conclusion that: 'The Soviet political system, when conceived as a monolith, is a myth'.

It would not be undeserved to dismiss the entire study by pointing out that it is hard to believe that by computerising 24,000 paragraphs from eleven official Soviet journals one can arrive at the conclusion that the Soviet political system is competitive and that its monolithism is a myth. But as we are here concerned with the usefulness and feasibility of contents-quantifying with communist official data in Western researches, it is useful to look, if only briefly, into the more profound reasons why this type of study could not lead to valid assessments.

First of all the terms of reference were confusing. The principal term, élite, was not defined explicitly – and implicitly was made to consist of five groups insufficiently representative (legal élite) or arbitrarily characterised (the 'collective nouns' chosen for the literary élite were: 'workers in culture', 'writers', 'artists', and '(literary) (?) editors'). Nor were the concepts of 'participatory attitudes' defined (on the contrary they were confused constantly with 'critical attitudes') or of 'party–élite relations' (for which no attempt was made to disentangle the mixed loyalties of the person or groups of persons having a joint interest in the party and in the profession concerned).

Then periodisation was arbitrarily chosen (apart from being confusingly worded in the title: instead of *since Stalin* it should have been presumably *since Stalin's death*). On the one hand, relations between party and 'élites' had already shown changes before Stalin rose to sole power (the first seven post-revolutionary, Leninist, years offer great scope for this kind of study). On the other hand, during the Stalinist period, the years 1929–36 were the most propitious for the 'economic élite', the years 1941–4 for the 'military élite'. Finally, after Stalin's death, different relations with different 'élites' were established by the party (a) during the years of Malenkov's ascendancy, (b) during the years of Khrushchev's domination, and (c) since the coming to power of Brezhnev and Kosygin. Thus to detect only one 'trend' since Stalin's death is unwarranted.

Further, the source-material proposed for the research was (a) insufficient, as the author acknowledged (number of paragraphs, number of journals, mechanical intabulations of 'collective nouns' and other such devices), and (b) particularly unrepresentative for the subject of the research. Indeed, the specialist journals in the U.S.S.R., which are particularly restrained and controlled on general political or major public issues, are encouraged to adopt a parochial professional attitude. This was constantly confused in the research with 'group-consciousness'.

There was also *ab initio* a total discrepancy between the meagreness and inadequacy of the empirical 'data' to be analysed, and the 'hypotheses' to which it was hoped the analysis might provide the answers. There are no grounds at all to believe that major political questions could be examined through this politically unrepresentative material. Had the study been limited to *professional*, functional attitudes, the material should have been much more specialised (*all* professional journals of *one* well-defined profession: dentists, accountants, industrial managers, advocates); but, then, in any case, no major political conclusions could have been expected to be drawn from it.

Moreover the inquiry, as directed, overlooked two special circumstances which were bound to run counter to the general premise which it posited. One is that in communist states the professional pride or self-consciousness of such categories as lawyers of writers is stressed precisely when the party asks them to make further and more abject political concessions. In the case of the writers this is a well-known tactic: the more the Writers' Union is being pressurised to denounce a writer such as Pasternak or Solzhenitsyn, the more it will stress publicly its independence of action, and ask the government and the party to show its respect for and interest in the profession. Thus the numbers of 'professional' paragraphs will rapidly increase as a price for the few paragraphs doing the dirty job against one or more members in political conflict with the party. The other circumstance is that the analysis did not take into account the internecine rivalries and intrigues within the 'élite' professions themselves. The lack of discrimination between the attitudes of individuals or internal sub-groups of the alleged 'élites', more often than not fighting for the favours of the party, greatly hampered the analytical prospects.

Finally, there was *ab initio* a lack of plausibility in the suggestion that such meagre research material could ever be relevant for major political hypotheses. The most that this unrepresentative material could achieve was to confirm, through its doubtful micro-channels, well-known developments amply observed through macro-channels of information. One did not need to analyse 24,000 paragraphs from professional journals to conclude that since Stalin's death, and in the wake of the increasing pluralisation of the industrial society of the U.S.S.R., the C.P.S.U. has had to maintain better relations with the technical intelligentsia, with the army or with the economists. On the contrary it was the

23

'hypotheses' set from the beginning which, it was hoped, would be corroborated by yet another range of empirical data. (That the ultimate purpose of the technique of the study was to make its findings coincide with political truisms is shown also in the frequent incidental political conclusions drawn in the work, as for instance: 'Although not readily apparent from the figures, Marshal Zhukov's removal in 1957 was a crucial development in *apparatchiki*–military relations.')

The overall conclusion is that in so far as it is of the essence of analysis by quantification to be saturated with genuine first-hand data, such studies undertaken by Western researchers succeed only in cases where the research can be carried out on genuinely firsthand and representative communist data.

B. RECONCEPTUALISATION

Political scientists like Carl Friedrich, W. Robson, Karl Loewenstein, Roy Macridis, Karl Deutsch, S. E. Finer, Gunnar Heckscher, S. Beer and, last but not least, Giovanni Sartori, have sought, in the forties and early fifties, to find new lines along which political analysis could be made to delve more deeply into the reality of the political processes than did the formal constitutional or institutional analysis. They were trying to find a 'systematic frame for comparative analysis' (Roy C. Macridis) so as to allow the former studies of comparative government 'to assume the character of a total science if it is to serve as a conscious instrument of social engineering' (1944 Report of the American Political Science Association). This somewhat utopian attempt to reconceptualise the political theory and transform it into a *science* still remains the unattained, and perhaps unattainable, goal of comparative politics. In general, as already mentioned, the discipline is still at the exhortatory phase.

The institution which has helped most towards the rallying of individual comparative approaches under one general methodological umbrella, however elastic, is the Committee for Comparative Politics of the American Social Science Research Council. It was due to the initiative of that committee that vast programmes of teamwork for studies in comparative politics were launched. Some outstanding work was immediately achieved, leaving behind the sterile critical-exhortatory phase. On the basis of this work the merits and demerits, advantages and disadvantages, and chances and risks of the method, became easier to discern. At the same time, the impulse given to such interests led to the flourishing, especially in the United States, of new and original approaches, linked with the names of leading political scientists – David Easton, Gabriel Almond, Robert A. Dahl, David Apter, Harry Eckstein, Lucian Pye, Sidney Verba, David Coleman, Powell, etc. The studies in political sociology carried out under the guidance of S. M. Lipset and Stein Rokkan have formed yet another tributary of the large stream of comparative politics.

This operation of reconceptualisation naturally spread afterwards to the field of communist studies. The communist régimes had to be included, and explained, within the 'global theory' of contemporary politics. From both sides, that of the political scientists in quest of comprehensive frameworks and that of the sovietologists in quest of a comparative method, attempts were soon made to join forces.

ALMOND'S 'POLITICAL CAPABILITIES' FOR COMPARATIVE COMMUNISM

David Easton's work is the most coherent and imaginative attempt to embrace all political phenomena in one general synthesis. Moreover, it is in Easton's work that some of the most important elements of systematic analysis were first proposed, such as, for instance, the notion of systems-analysis itself, or the basic conception of inputs and outputs in the functioning of a polity. Yet, perhaps because his scheme is too abstract, Easton's work did not *directly* attract the interest of the 'practitioners' in the field of comparative communist politics. (This is a pity, because Easton's theory of ideology as a legitimising factor is, to take only one example, extremely relevant and fruitful for the interpretation of communist régimes.) Instead Gabriel Almond's work proved to be more accessible and popular. As a practical animator and inspirer of various schemes and programmes Almond was at the centre of activity of the Committee for Comparative Politics. As a theoretical populariser he was, on the one hand, responsible, alone or with others such as Coleman, Powell, Verba and Pye, for elaborating simultaneously or successively, complementarily or contradictorily, the most cogent comparative political formulae, as, for instance, 'political capabilities', 'political development', 'political culture', 'civic culture', etc. On the other hand, by adopting and adapting David Easton's initial element of inputs (demands and supports) and outputs (authoritative decisions), Almond provided a more detailed framework of comparative analysis. He divided the input element into four functions: political socialisation and recruitment, interest articulation, interest aggregation, and political communication; and the output element into three functions: rule-making, rule-application and rule-adjudication.

This was in a sense an operation in *renaming* the old concepts of political theory so as to make them fit the non-institutional approaches of political sociology or indeed sociology (Talcott Parsons's pattern-variables). But nevertheless it was this Almondian scheme of the seven inputs and outputs which has probably proved to be the most popular framework yet for comparative communist studies. It reconciled most of the comparative students specialising in communist affairs who were asked to join in global comparative studies.

Thus the American Frederick C. Barghoorn (*Politics in the U.S.S.R.*):[24]

> For anyone who seeks indicators of possible changes in the political system's performance, Almond's key-concept is 'political capabilities'. These are shaped by the 'input' of demands and supports fed into the polity and by the latter's corresponding 'output' of policy. Even at the present state of our knowledge the 'systems' approach has the merit of sensitising our thinking to change. Changes in the Soviet polity have occurred in startling profusion and promise to occur with increasing rapidity.

Or the Australian T. H. Rigby (*Communist Party Membership in the U.S.S.R. 1917–1967*):[25]

> . . . the framework we shall employ here is a fairly radical adaptation of that proposed by Gabriel Almond. The work of

Almond and his co-authors represents a major step forward in the comparative study of political systems. Several of their concepts and insights are of considerable value in the study of Soviet political processes.

Or the British David Lane (*Politics and Society of the U.S.S.R.*):[26] 'Let us begin with a definition of the political system. It has been defined by Gabriel Almond as . . .' and further : 'The political system of modern societies may be considered in terms of demands and supports, the articulation of inputs, the aggregation of interests, output and enforcement. . . . How can we adapt this "systems" model to the Soviet political system ?'

It is true that once these three authors, chosen here for the fact that they come from three different continents, had made their statement of allegiance, each proceeded, as Lane said, to see how the model could be applied to the Soviet political system. This produced, in the quite sizeable number of such studies, a sizeable number of variations on the theme. All these variations suffered, more often than not, from an inevitable lack of precision. But then this is true of most of the individual authors, or groups of authors, who experiment with new methodological terms. The important fact was not the number, ingeniousness or quality of the variations, but the fact that the comparative models had produced a trend towards methodological unification for the authors and researchers, working until then in isolation in their separate areas of monographs. This conversion of the younger students of communist affairs to a general framework of political analysis started the present trend towards re-grouping communist comparative studies around one or another comparative concept : development, groups, bureaucracy, etc.

THE DEVELOPMENTAL COMMUNIST STUDIES

During the important reconsideration which took place at the Symposium on Comparative Politics and Communist Systems held in 1966, Alfred Meyer wrote : 'Some beginnings have been made with attempts to account for Communist experiences by fitting them into models of modernisation. We are beginning to be aware also of the need for studying the structuring effect which the industrial economy and the social psychology of industrial life have on political systems'; and John H. Kautsky added: '. . . more particularly I should like to express my agreement with what I think is implied throughout Professor Meyer's paper, that is that Communist and general comparative studies should be integrated in a developmental framework. . . . I would suggest, then, that Communist revolutions, including the Russian revolution, be placed, for analytical purposes, in the context of revolution in underdeveloped countries.'[27] This new orientation was in part a reflection of the growing influence of development studies on comparative politics as a whole[28] but it was also the revival of the analysis of the communist phenomenon by the study of the impact of their economic development on given communist societies. No serious studies of individual or groups of communist countries had overlooked, for instance, the impact which the stages and trends of industrialisation had, and can have, on the political processes of those states.

Looking back into the early history of the comparative-development approach to communist studies, and its crystallisation as a reaction against the uniform totalitarian approach, one should probably situate at the very beginning P. Sorokin's *Sociological System*,[29] James Burnham's *The Managerial Revolution*[30] and more directly W. W. Rostow's method of analysis described in his book *The Process of Economic Growth*.[31] The model proposed by W. W. Rostow, an economist, suffered inevitably, when projected on to political problems, from over-simplification.

One of the first studies of the interaction of the 'stages of economic growth' with communist politics was effected by W. W. Rostow himself in his book *The Dynamics of Soviet Society*.[32] The inquiry adopted the view 'that even in a modern totalitarian society such interaction takes place', and proceeded to 'examine the balance of forces within the expectations of men and the working of certain key institutions'. It found out, as it proceeded, that there was general popular dissatisfaction, but it also proceeded to look further into the more diversified and specialised study of 'group dissatisfaction'. However, obviously because of the lack of empirical data, the examination of the 'dissatisfied groups' was limited to the peasantry, the national minorities, the intellectuals, the middle and lower bureaucrats, the industrial workers and, oddly enough, 'the prison and forced labour' groups. Each of these was given only a few pages.

Instead there was a much longer section of 'conclusions' which endeavoured to take stock of the position within the Soviet Union at the interim date of 15 May 1953, and, in particular, to assess the forces then at work shaping the Soviet future – thus keeping the pledge given in the introduction that the 'analysis is also meant to assist the making of American policy'. However, from an academic point of view Rostow's book situated itself half-way between the general purpose of comparative politics – to try to 'predict' – and the more special position taken by practitioners (or analysts) whose deductions are expected to be of help to governmental agencies. Some of these studies undertook to link the vague and inchoate 'groups' within the Soviet Union with individual Soviet political leaders allegedly engaged in rivalry for power, and allegedly backed by politically identifiable 'groups' in industrial communist society.

Also deriving from Burnham's *Managerial Revolution* – and from Rostow's theory of economic growth – was the assumption of the convergence of the Western, especially the American, and the communist, especially the Soviet, industrial-technological societies. The idea that the basic structures of the previously antagonistic (at least from an ideological point of view) systems are drawing together because of the imperative common laws of all industrial societies continues to preoccupy even today such professionally and politically differing authors as the economists J. K. Galbraith, J. Tinbergen, Peter Wiles, Jan S. Prybyla, or E. Mandel; the political scientists, the late Peter Nettl or Alfred Meyer (about whose work on the theory of convergence of advanced industrial societies *qua* industrial organisations or especially bureaucracies, more will be said in the second part); and the sociologists, Raymond Aron or N. Birnbaum.

Yet Raymond Aron, the sociologist whose special subject matter is industrial societies, gave an explicit warning against this inference to be made from the theory of 'stages':

W. W. Rostow has distinguished four stages of growth. . . . But the object of the comparison is to bring out the differences as much as to emphasise the similarities. It would be a pity if

29

we now transformed the idea of stages of growth, which in itself is useful, and attempted to explain and predict everything in these terms. The idea that the Soviet and Western societies are gradually drawing closer together and tending towards a mixed form is, at the most, only a hypothesis.[33]

The same sceptical conclusion on convergence was drawn also by S. P. Huntington and Z. Brzezinski at the end of their cross-area comparative study, limited to the two super-powers (the U.S.A. and the U.S.S.R.), *Political Power: U.S.A./U.S.S.R.*[34]

New Left authors, with near-Trotskyist, quasi-Maoist approaches, like the economist E. Mandel, the sociologist N. Birnbaum and, last but not least, the philosopher H. Marcuse, have based their theories on the basic similarities and on the obvious convergence of the U.S.A. and the U.S.S.R., or generally speaking of the capitalist and state-capitalist technological societies; whereas the official media in the U.S.S.R. took a strong stand against the 'Western theory of convergence'.[35]

THE STUDY OF GROUPS

The study of groups in communist societies has a double origin. The first is the revival of studies of groups in political theory initiated under the influence of Bentley[36] and Laski[37] at the beginning of the century, and generalised in modern political science through such works as David Truman's *The Governmental Process.*[38] By now the pluralistic view of society is generally accepted in Western modern political science and especially political sociology. Indeed, though originally a subdivision of the major body of political science, political sociology became for a while the tail which wagged the entire dog. Through the obvious advantages it enjoyed in its empirical research, it tried to proclaim the emergent discipline of political science as a subdivision of sociology.

Be that as it may, the fact is that in comparative communist studies the study of groups met with an immediate success, as it offered, on the one hand, a field of hard empirical research and, on the other, a welcome reaction to the static totalitarian approaches.

But the second source of this kind of study was to be found in the communist countries themselves, and especially in Poland, Hungary and Czechoslovakia where progressive sociologists and political sociologists saw in this technique the fulfilment of their desire to introduce into the fossilised historical-materialist approach the living reality of empirical research. The notions of 'groupism' (or 'grupovshchina') and 'pluralism' were only waiting for a little academic freedom in some of the communist countries (it is to be noticed that in the U.S.S.R. the social sciences are still *anti*-pluralistic) to become one of the principal research approaches of the schools of sociology and political science, reopened in some communist countries. This provided in the sixties one of the most useful bridges between similar studies being undertaken in Western and communist countries.

The main disillusionment provoked by this otherwise most successful approach remains still the elusiveness and mercurial nature of the categories of groups and the difficulties of obtaining in general, and more especially in the field of communist studies, more order in the categories around which comparative studies could be polarised. The reasons why Rostow's division of groups in 1953 (quoted above) proved unsatisfactory have been mentioned. Yet one is struck by the lack of progress, during these particularly active years in the study of groups, in the essential work of classification and clarification. The same vagueness in definition, timidity in delineation, leading to overlapping, and above all the absence of firm criteria for categorising, continue to affect this otherwise constructive approach.

The permanent difficulty underlying all attempts to classify the groups in communist societies for comparative purposes was perhaps best described in a recent summing-up by H. Gordon Skilling, a pioneer of such studies since the fifties :

One might, for instance, classify groups in terms of the techniques of action employed. . . . One might differentiate between groups whose main purpose was a positive influence on the outcome of policy, and those whose purpose was the negative one of preventing official policy from being carried out. One might weigh the relative significance of groups based on occupational or other social distinctions and those based on common opinion. One might also, of course, evaluate the relative importance and effectiveness of political groups in attaining their ends under various conditions. These and other studies would not only contribute to a more precise knowledge of the nature of group conflict in Communist systems but also provide a tool for more precisely differentiating these systems from each other, as well as from those in the non-Communist world.[39]

The hopeful but yet characteristically vague and timid tone of these remarks, by an author who some seven years ago pioneered this methodological approach, form a melancholy warning for those who believe that the study of groups, by itself, can provide an exclusive approach to studies of comparative communism.

BUREAUCRACY

The studies in bureaucracy have been inspired directly by the Weberian and post-Weberian theoretical alignment of the major studies of politics around the concepts of bureaucracy and bureaucratisation, as well as by the Trotskyite and post-Trotskyite denunciation of the 'bureaucratisation of the revolution'. They have the advantage of offering a firm basis for comparative evaluation. Although the notion was present also in the 'totalitarian' studies, the original and modern approach to the study of communist bureaucracy consists in separating it from the terror, clumsiness, cruelty and arbitrariness of Stalinist totalitarianism. It aims now rather at studying bureaucracy in its impersonal characteristics of efficiency and, indeed, 'rationality'. Bureaucracy is the institution which, *pace* Weber, is thought to be common and central to all forms of politics and which interests those modern comparative students who want to situate their analysis in the middle of the spectrum of all shades and nuances of the typology of states.

Thus, as a sequel to this thinking along the line of bureaucracy as the new common denominator, new adjectives began to be used for describing the modern, or industrial, communist societies. Allen Kassoff coined the expression 'The Administered Society: Totalitarianism without Terror';[40] T. H. Rigby proposed the 'organisational' or 'command-dominated' concept; Paul Cocks[41] spoke of 'the rationalisation of party control', using the concept of

32

rationalisation in almost Weberian terms. But it was still the mercurial Alfred J. Meyer who, in his 1967 essay on 'The Comparative Study of Communist Political Systems',[42] made the point explicitly and tried to explain the entire approach in plain terms :

> I have argued in recent works that at least one communist system can be understood adequately by comparing it with complex modern bureaucratic organisations anywhere. Like modern bureaucracy, communist rule is essentially an attempt to impose rational management over social life by means of complex organisations.

And in his essay on 'Theories of Convergence' :[43]

> The Soviet Union can best be understood as a giant bureaucracy, something like a modern corporation extended over the entire society, or a 'General Motors writ large'. It is remarkable that the Soviet textbook definition of socialism is almost exactly the same as the Weberian and post-Weberian definition of bureaucracy.

One can see from these two sample quotations the advantage of a recognisable and well-defined concept and a universally valid institution for a proper comparative study. But by the same token one can also see the exaggerations to which such a comparative approach can lead if and when it is not anchored in the sounder political definitions. But of this at greater length in the second part of this survey.

The conclusions that one can draw from this summary survey of the progress made by conceptual communist studies is that, on the positive side, these studies have finally succeeded in extricating the study of communist politics from the limits of sovietology and linking it honourably and profitably with the main orientations and trends of social science in general. Communist political studies are now integrated in the main body; from both sides of the previous gap, that of the classic social sciences and that of the peripheral descriptive, monographic or historical studies of countries under communist régimes, a solid *rapprochement* has now been established. Indeed it is hoped that, for instance, another major trend of comparative studies, that inspired by the theory of communication, will be successfully applied to the field of communist studies as well.

But at the same time, and above all, it can be inferred that *all* the techniques of the systemic approach should be used together. The difficulties of research in communist studies are such that to experiment with only one approach, or to link everything to one approach, would be counter-productive. Mixed studies of bureaucracy, groups, communication, and combined techniques of quantification, behaviourism, and other approaches, checked against each other and summed up in fair generalisations, is as much as one can hope for from the present state of comparative communist methods. Even then, as will be shown in the second part of this survey, the result, if not linked with major *political* concepts, would be insufficient for drawing direct *political* conclusions.

On the debit side of the ledger two major critical observations should be made. One is that whereas conceptual comparative communist studies have been more successful in constructing global, cross-area, schemata, and integrating either one individual state (more frequently the U.S.S.R.) or an abstract ideal-type of communist polity in these universal projections, they have signally failed to make a similar progress in intra-area comparative studies. What was won in universalist generalisations was lost[44] in the possibility of furthering comparative studies of the different *types* of communist polities, ranging now as widely as from China through the U.S.S.R. to Yugoslavia, Czechoslovakia and Hungary. And yet it is in these differences, and their nuances and gradings, that the greatest hope lies for an understanding of the comparative aspects of communist politics. Perhaps the conceptual studies were too much in their infancy and too deeply engaged in their spectacular methodological polemics, brandishing one concept after another and one 'key' after another, to attempt to examine the intra-area aspects. But there may also be another, more worrying, reason. This is that the methodological tools of the universalistic conceptual studies might be too blunt and too abstractly vague for the other, more delicate, but precise work of comparative analysis and evaluation.

The second is that, generally speaking, all the work undertaken up to now in allegedly *comparative politics*, as it was called in the early days, has in reality been of greater service to *sociology*, via *political sociology*, than to the study of *politics* and, in our case, of communist politics. But it is precisely this question which forms the backbone of the argument put forward in the second section of this survey.

2. THE COMPARATIVE STUDY OF THE SOCIALIST STATE

The moment has now come to explain the contention which was implicit in the preceding critical recapitulation. This is that the concept of the state is still useful for comparative political studies. This does not mean that a debate should be reopened here on whether the study of the state is still the pivot of political science. Nor does this mean that this is the only approach that can be recommended; or that the great advances in reconceptualisation, made in the last decade, are denied.[45] What is argued here is that the concept of the state is particularly present in the field of communist comparative politics. This is so because the socialist states are the most organised and the most centralised of all contemporary states; because in so far as from the point of view of communist doctrine the communist state is both a provisional institution and an ideological anomaly, its study offers a direct comparative insight into the communist theories and practices themselves; and because in so far as the very existence of all contemporary states, as sovereign units and as centralistic political institutions, is questioned in the light of the evolution of the industrial society, the socialist states must be examined from this vantage-point together and comparatively with all contemporary states.

PRESENCE OF THE CONCEPT

The attempts to eliminate, ignore or replace completely the concept of the state in comparative political studies have failed.

This is not the place to open the general discussion on the need for and importance of the concept of the state in modern political science as a whole. This is being debated in American political science as well as in Britain by authors of recent comparative

36

government studies such as S. E. Finer or Jean Blondel.[46] Perhaps Harry Eckstein's remarks of 1963 (in his introduction to Harry Eckstein and David Apter, *Comparative Politics: A Reader*, New York, 1963) best sum up this unsolved dilemma of political science:

> Political scientists knew the proper subject matter of their science: the state. . . . Today precisely because of the variety of approaches in the field we are not at all sure about these and other basic matters. Yet the most obvious way to limit political inquiry is to focus on the *most obviously political thing there is,* as political scientists did in the formative years of their field, namely formal-legal structure. [*our italics*]

But this is the place to show that especially in comparative communist politics the use of the concept of the state is so necessary that the more the sub-discipline broadens its specific gauges, the more this basic concept reasserts itself. In two of the most recent, and therefore better articulated, attempts to establish a comparative communist framework, the determination to elude or replace the concept of the state by others became pathetically obvious and proved, if anything, their futility.

Thus in Chalmers Johnson (ed.), *Change in Communist Systems* (Stanford, 1970), the editor and rapporteur of the study-group defines the methodology of the study as 'comparing Communist nations'. It thus drops the embarrassing 'systems' from the title, but retains from the concept of nation-state only the first, and presumably less controversial, half. This only makes matters worse. For it is not the *nations* of the communist world, in an ethnic context, that the study intends to compare, but the communist *nation-states* and their respective position in the diversity of the *political* spectrum. This is readily confirmed by the author: 'Diversity', he says, 'comes from the very fact that Communist political systems exist as national states in an age when global politics is still seen as a system of relations among such states'.[47] Yet for reasons of methodological fashionability, the full concept of communist state is not manfully grasped, but the surrogates, 'system' or 'nation', timidly introduced and at once withdrawn.

The other example is that of Alfred Meyer, already encountered in this survey as a pioneering student of comparative communism, when he introduces bureaucracy as the key-concept for this kind of comparative studies. 'Like modern bureaucracy', he says, 'Communist rule is essentially an attempt to impose rational management over social life by means of complex organisations.' But no sooner is this abstract framework constructed upon all modern bureaucracies 'from General Motors to the U.S.S.R.' than Meyer immediately makes the rejoinder: '. . . Communist systems look remarkably similar to bureaucratic organisations in other parts of the world. An important difference which remains is that the Communist systems are sovereign bureaucracies, whereas other bureaucracies exist and operate within larger societal frameworks so that a Communist state becomes one single bureaucratic system extended over the entire society, or bureaucracy writ large.'[48] Here again, as in the previous case of Chalmers Johnson, it is obvious that what the author is talking about is the communist states, indeed sovereign states, and their specific features, one of them being, of course, the bureaucratic organisation. But here again, for reasons of methodological conformism, the concept of the state is introduced only furtively and only at the very last and inevitable moment of the comparison.

TREBLE JUSTIFICATION OF THE USE OF THE CONCEPT IN COMPARATIVE COMMUNIST POLITICS

In so far as socialism is the system in which the means of production are owned and controlled by the state, and in so far as according to Marxist-Leninist definition and terminology the revolutionary building-up of communism has now reached the stage of *socialist states* but not as yet, anywhere, the stage of communist *society* or *societies*, the concept of the state and of its relationship to society is central to the understanding of the political problems of contemporary communism. It can even be said that it is today more relevant to the understanding of the communist political system than it is to that of other political systems.

This is so for three reasons: first, as has already been explained, because they are all 'states' the socialist states offer themselves *qua states* to objective comparison, both from the cross-area point of view with other non-socialist states, and from the intra-area point of view with other socialist states, as groups of socialist states which differ among themselves, by one or more characteristics, within the common, ideological context.

Then, the concept of the state is particularly relevant to the analysis of the politics of the socialist states precisely because its permanent existence is *in principle* denied by the socialist ideology (or ideologies). The state itself ought to be dissolved in the communist society. The socialist state is accepted in theory only as the embodiment of the transitional period of the dictatorship of the proletariat during which the previous bourgeois state is being 'smashed'. The permanent establishment of the state and of its central institutions is, therefore, contrary to the very essence of socialism which is synonymous with complete decentralisation, self-administration, and lack of controls. Herewith we are able to use the comparative vantage-point of the controversy between the three major schools of thought of contemporary Marxism-Leninism.

Finally, in the light of the changing character of the technological-industrial society (and the U.S.S.R. and most European socialist states are in this category), the study of the relations between the central institution, and above all of the central government, and the essentially centrifugal and pluralised societies, is essential. Will the state survive this modern test, or will it give way to other political institutions? The study of the socialist states, the most centralised states in existence, is highly relevant from this point of view as well.

A. COMPARABILITY OF THE SOCIALIST STATES

(a) Cross-area

The socialist states have three principal features in common with most other states.

SOVEREIGNTY

The socialist states are defined as the bearers of their own sovereignty, i.e. internal and external sovereignty.

The first socialist state was founded on 10 July 1918 as the 'Russian Socialist Federal Soviet Republic'. This (and its successor, which became in 1923 a component part of the Union of

Soviet Socialist Republics, formed on 6 July 1923) replaced, after eight months of hesitation, the Russian state and empire suspended on 7 November 1917. The hesitation was caused by the problem crucial to the communist (and anarcho-syndicalist) revolutionaries in power of whether the new political structure should resemble that of the Commune of Paris, and be, as the Commissar of Justice, Reissner, proposed in January 1918, a 'federation of social-economic organisations', when he directly opposed and denounced 'an alliance of territorial governments and states'. The 'territorial' solution prevailed and the new sovereign state was thus born and expanded into the federation of the U.S.S.R. which, in spite of its territorial vastness and multinationality, was defined by its constitution as 'a single federal state'. Since then all other socialist states (socialist republics or people's democracies) proclaimed in the meantime – Outer Mongolia (1940), Yugoslavia (1945), Bulgaria (1946), Albania (1946), Hungary (1946), Romania (1946), Poland (1947), Czechoslovakia (1948), China (1949), German Democratic Republic (1949), North Korea (1948), North Vietnam (1960), Cuba (1961) – are defined in their constitutions as sovereign states. The problem of sovereignty with its twin external and internal aspects is relevant to the understanding of the political problems of these states.

The concept of external sovereignty regulates the relations between socialist states. The Soviet doctrine has taken endless pains to distinguish between the two kinds of relations. A socialist state is fully sovereign in relation to all other states. But in relations among socialist states, in so far as sovereignty in socialist doctrine should be viewed also as a class-concept, and in so far as all socialist states are states of the working class, the fact that the working class *is international* should colour in a different way the general aspect of the sovereignty of the respective states. The ambiguity of this approach has made the Soviet doctrine oscillate constantly between offensive phases when it stresses especially international socialism, with its corollary: subordination of other socialist states to the guidance and care of the U.S.S.R.; and defensive phases when it stresses, under pressure from the other socialist states, the unchallengeable sovereignty of any state in any situation. To take two recent examples: the declaration of 31 October 1956 on the commonwealth of socialist states insisted on the independence and full sovereignty of each of these states in relations with any such states and especially the U.S.S.R.; but the 'Brezhnev doctrine', elaborated immediately before and after the invasion of Czechoslovakia in 1968, stressed on the contrary the right of other socialist states, and primarily the U.S.S.R., to intervene in the affairs of another socialist state, when it is thought that that state is in danger of losing its socialist integrity. The Soviet doctrine is opposed by the doctrine of sovereignty of most other socialist states, but especially by that of Yugoslavia, Albania, China, and Romania.

The concept of internal sovereignty takes us into the range of problems of the central government, controls, authority and coercion. This is a doubly acute problem in the socialist states: (a) *qua* soviet- or commune-states which should have from their very inception devolved all power to the decentralised social and economic associations and should never have established central control, and (b) *qua* modern, industrialised societies in quest of efficiency through participation of the producer in the process of production. This is, as will be shown, the principal question for the interpretation of communist comparative politics, i.e. whether, how, and for how long will any of the contemporary socialist states *be able* to maintain the present over-centralised, monolithic, state-structure?

REPRESENTATIVE GOVERNMENT

Like most modern non-socialist states, the socialist states base their legitimacy on the representativeness of their institutions.[49] The political principle of their sovereignty is that it embodies the 'will of the people' or of the 'working people'. The political expression of the will of the people is ensured by the representation of the electorate in the representative bodies at all levels, from the local soviets, national committees, people's councils, etc., to the supreme soviets, national assemblies or federal chambers. To be sure, most of the constitutions and political theories of the socialist states acknowledge unhesitatingly the element of selective representation as their *political* bloodstream. But they interpret this as a transitional phase until the unanimous forms of direct administration, self-management and social organisations

41

should replace the political institutions. Yet such an interpretation first forms a vicious circle, for what is said here is that as long as there are socialist states the institutions of these states will claim to be representative; and, then, there is no evidence, even in the most utopian descriptions of the society of the future, that the element of representation will be totally discarded. On the contrary, it appears that in the passage from utopian revolutionary desiderata to practical applications the Russian and other communist revolutions have lost much less time in accepting the inevitability of representation than did the French or American revolutions in their quest for the 'unanimity' and 'permanence' of the people's deliberation and decision-making.

Western political science has naturally and necessarily taken great pains to demonstrate that the alleged representative institutions of the socialist states are not sufficiently, or not at all, representative, as they do not emanate from free elections with their *sine qua non* prerequisites: free suffrage, choice of candidates, independent judiciary, freedom of organisation for political parties competing for power, etc. This, of course, is very important. But it is also important to see that, vitiated or unreal though they may be, it is still on the representative mediation that the political structure of those states is built and not on the institutions of direct self-management, which were thought to be specific to socialism.

PARTIES

Like that of most non-socialist states (with the exception of those states in which the army has assumed power directly, or those states in which, owing to the general political amorphousness, political parties have not yet come into existence) the government of the socialist states is exercised by one political party in power. The institution of the political party, although functioning in totally different conditions from those in the non-socialist states, is particularly powerful in the socialist states where constitutional checks and balances of other institutions are reduced to a minimum.

The ways of contrasting the communist parties in power in the socialist states with the political parties in the non-socialist states

42

are understandably numerous, and the differences understandably obvious. The former are defined as: monolithic, single- or one-party, non-competitive, dictatorial, repressive or, last but not least, totalitarian; the latter as: pluralistic, multi-party, electoral-competitive, alternating, expressive or democratic. Perhaps one of the most direct comparisons can be obtained by observing that whereas most contemporary states have parties of government, the socialist states have no parties of opposition (or, to be more precise, have no parties which can compete overtly in free elections for power – for in Poland, the G.D.R. or China, for instance, several parties still exist).

In so far as the role and the future of the communist party *qua* single party of government is a central question for the analysis of the socialist states, more will naturally be said in this survey about this institution. Here let it be noted that with the above qualifications the party is yet another institution common to most contemporary states.

(b) Intra-area

It is suggested that all socialist states have in common at least the following five characteristics which they do not share with the non-socialist states: (i) most of them are born out of war; (ii) they own the means of production within their territories; (iii) they are teleological; (iv) they are apparat states; (v) they are oppositionless.

WAR-ORIGINS

All socialist states have come into being in the aftermath of a war – with the exception of Cuba. By this is meant that: (a) socialist states have as a rule superseded other states which collapsed during a war, and (b) socialist states have generally built their central structures, in Jacobin fashion (usually starting with the army, the police, economic controls, etc.), usually during the effort of war or as a direct aftermath of war.

But this being said, it is important to observe immediately that there are three different ways in which war has been the origin of the socialist states – and that this has had a direct impact on (*a*) the ideology of the party in power, and (*b*) on the relations between the socialist states.

(i) The R.S.F.S.R., and subsequently the U.S.S.R., was born out of the collapse of the Russian Tsarist Empire in the First World War. The revolutionary Bolshevik Party came to power because of the implicit conditions of political vacuum created by this collapse, but also explicitly because of the popular response which its anti-war campaign obtained from the Russian people. Moreover, as the socialist parties in Western Europe had made themselves guilty of association with the national war-efforts of their respective countries, the Russian Bolshevik Party took the lead in forming a Third International of communist parties distinct from the others also by their absolute internationalism and pacifism. Later, since the formation of a socialist state 'in one country', but especially during and after the Second World War, the internationalist-pacifist aspect of the communist ideology was replaced by the nationalist-imperialist ideology of the Soviet government.

(ii) The Federative People's Republic of Yugoslavia, the People's Republic of Albania, and the People's Republic of China, replaced the previous Yugoslav, Albanian and Chinese states during and after a war of liberation of their territories from the occupation by foreign invaders. The communist party managed, by way of direct military actions against the occupiers, as well as by waging a civil war against other national organisations, to take the lead in this war of liberation. This had as a direct consequence the fact that the ideology of the respective communist parties was transformed from the initial internationalist-pacifist into a national communism. Another consequence of this fact was that for a long time the respective communist parties fused with, and were eclipsed by, the Army of Liberation. (This, for instance, had lasting effects on the political institutions of China where the party and the army had never been as clearly separated as in the other socialist states.) Finally, it was natural that these three states should be the most eager to defend their sovereignty against any powers, including and especially the U.S.S.R. (and, in the case of Albania, including and especially Yugoslavia).

(iii) The People's Republics of Poland, Romania, Bulgaria, Hungary, the German Democratic Republic, and to some extent also Czechoslovakia, replaced the previous states over parts or the whole of their territories because of the passage of the Soviet armies through these territories and the dominant position obtained for this and other reasons by the U.S.S.R. over the parts of Europe formed by these territories. The Soviet government, using its direct and indirect dominance in that part of Europe, put and maintained in power the 'friendly' governments of the communist parties which transformed the respective states into socialist states (a notion which comprises equally the 'people's republic' and the 'socialist republics' – Romania and Czechoslovakia). This historical circumstance had a direct effect on the ideology of the respective communist parties, constantly torn between an instinctive 'national communism' and the superior Soviet-inspired 'socialist internationalism'. It also had a direct effect on the relations between these states and the U.S.S.R., and among these states themselves, according to whether their own national communism was better adapted, as in the case of the Polish, Bulgarian and the German socialist states, to the Soviet-sponsored internationalism, or, as in the case of the Romanian, Hungarian or Czechoslovak, to the direct defence of their sovereignty against everybody. The case of Cuba needs to be studied at greater length and in the special context of Latin America.

Also, more recently, the possibility has opened for the coming to power of communist parties, in alliance with other parties, by means of elections. The case of Allende in Chile is, of course, the most striking example of such a situation – and ought to be relevant to comparative prognostications in the case of those West European countries where communist parties show an undiminished electoral strength, notably Italy and France. But in the present case of Chile, as well as in any future similar cases, the conceptual threshold, indeed Rubicon, to be observed is the moment when the institutions characteristic of the pluralist-constitutional state are abolished, and replaced by the institutions of the socialist state (or dictatorship of the proletariat), some of which will be described in the following points of this section.

Most socialist states have abolished all private ownership of means of production. In Yugoslavia and Poland the land still belongs to the farmers. In China the 1949 Organic Law still acknowledges the existence of four forms of ownership, the last two of which are 'ownership by individual working people and capitalist ownership'. But otherwise, by and large, and undoubtedly in the supremely important sections of industry and the public services, private ownership has been totally expropriated. This fact obviously conditions the social and political processes in the socialist states, links them together in a separate conceptual bracket, and distinguishes their processes from those of the non-socialist states.

But the measure of egalitarianism thus obtained by expropriation on the *economic* plane did not produce the instant political-social effects which were expected. First, the question 'Who now owns the property thus nationalised?' is unsatisfactorily answered. Second, differences in incomes, status and standards of living with their subsequent conflicts have reappeared unequivocally. Finally, not only have the perennial political structures, institutions, and processes not 'withered away', but new and weightier forms of political rule, hierarchy and subordination have become characteristic of the post-revolutionary society.

The answer to the first question is given differently in different socialist states. In the U.S.S.R. socialist property exists either in the form of 'state property' (belonging to the whole people), or in the form of 'co-operative and collective-farm property' (the property of collective farms or co-operative societies).[50] In Yugoslavia the notion is that of 'social ownership', the corollary of which is expressed as follows: 'Since no one has the right of ownership over the socially-owned means of production, the social-political community, or the working organisation or the working man, may not appropriate in any form of ownership the product of socially-organised work, nor manage and dispose of socially-owned means of production and work, nor arbitrarily determine the terms of distribution.'[51] This somehow negative definition is, however, the key to the system of Yugoslav self-management which, in turn, is of great importance to the Yugoslav socialist political system. The 1954 Chinese constitution, with its cautiously dialectical approaches, acknowledges 'at present'[52] the existence of four forms of ownership (the last two of which provide ownership by individual working men and capitalist ownership) and like the constitution of the U.S.S.R. equates state ownership with 'ownership by the whole people'. But both the Chinese and the Yugoslav communists challenge the Soviet idea of the control of the ownership of means of production, whether owned by the state or by no one. In their view, and in the view of the communist opposition to the Stalinist and post-Stalinist Soviet doctrine (and especially praxis), a new bureaucracy, or, in Djilas's terms, a 'new class', has monopolised the controls in the society and thus deprived the alleged 'ownership by the people' of any real meaning.

The answer to the political question, linked directly with the previous ones, will be discussed at greater length in the following subsections.

APPARAT STATES

All states have an apparatus or apparat. (This expression, in French *appareil*, is equivalent in German and Russian to the English notions of staff, administration and executive.) In dictatorial states the executive is neither accountable to the legislative nor can it be censured by the judiciary. But some dictatorial states can be described as apparat states.[53] These are the dictatorial states which are directed and controlled by one of the apparats or branches of the executive : the party, the armed forces or the political police. The ideology which any of these apparatus professes and implements before and after coming to power (social revolutionary for the party, nationalist revolutionary or conservative for the other two), justifies their leading role.

The expression 'apparat' was chosen because in communist terminology it describes the internal organisation of the communist party, the 'apparat' which after the coming to power is entrusted with guiding and controlling all the other apparats of the state (historically, this occurred in Soviet Russia at the Eighth [1919] and Ninth [1920] Congresses).

In contradistinction with the other states which claim to provide the community with the order and organisation necessary for it to function and to ensure the best conditions for its future prosperity, the socialist states are *teleological*. What is meant is that : (*a*) they serve a direct purpose – to transform society as well as the individuals in it by revolutionary means; (*b*) they describe themselves as transitional and purposefully destined to annihilate themselves; and (*c*) they also see this purpose contained and expressed in the ideology (that is the Marxist-Leninist ideology) which, by its constant inter-relation between its *theory* and *praxis*, is the actual motor of the transformation towards the final aim (*telos*) of the classless and apparatless society.

The political process of the socialist states cannot be understood without the permanent proviso of the ideological transformation, of the interplay between theory and praxis, between the changing and the changed, between the actual and the eventual. The talent for assessing each moment in the dialectic transformation of the three concentric circles (the world, the respective socialist state, and/or groups of socialist states) immediately and in their relation with the non-socialist states, and in the transformation, by socialisation of the human collectivities or masses moved, is the distinctive political mark of the leaders of such states. Like Lenin they are expected to interpret the changing situations while these are continuously changing, and to accelerate or relax the voluntary transformation accordingly.

The fact that this *deus ex machina* of the expropriation of the ownership of the means of production failed to produce instantly a total change in social relations, has brought new problems of organisation, order and hierarchy. The accent has since then understandably been laid on the progress of the transformation of men themselves, though in another economic context. In different senses and with different means the three major schools of thought of the Marxist-Leninist ideology – Soviet, Chinese and Yugoslav – agree on the primacy of the 'cultural' or 'political' or 'social' education of the masses. This long-term, and ultimately evolutionary, view of the parallel transformation of the objective institutions and of the subjective consciousness is the broadest justification of contemporary communist politics. But by the same token, this leads to the ardent controversies of interpretation within the Marxist-Leninist ideology. The concept of the 'dictatorship of the proletariat', the period during which the new state 'smashes' (*zerbrechen*) the old state so as to 'liberate' the classless, institutionless society, is understandably at the heart of the controversy. Whereas the Twenty-Second Congress of the C.P.S.U. has proclaimed that the passage from the 'dictatorship of the proletariat' to the 'state of the whole people' has been effected in the U.S.S.R., the Yugoslavs describe their own societal form as already a socialist federal community of working people . . . based on relations between people acting as free and equal producers and creators'. Yet the Chinese argue that in so far as differences and conflict of classes in the respective societies still exist in all socialist states, the dictatorship of the proletariat is still needed, and that 'to replace the state of the dictatorship of the proletariat by a state of a different character is nothing but a great historical retrogression'.[54]

OPPOSITIONLESS STATES

This is a comparative notion proposed by the author of this survey,[55] as a broad, cross-area, differentiation between pluralistic-constitutional states[56] and all other forms of state, especially socialist or nationalist dictatorships. The former are recognisable as a category of states within whose constitutional system political opposition is institutionalised and guaranteed. Political institutionalised opposition is seen as the right, and indeed obligation, of several political parties in the same state to *compete openly* for power by way of regular free elections, free communication and propaganda, public meetings, organisation and demonstrations, etc. Free elections, with their institutional activities, become themselves a prerequisite of the functioning of the institutionalised opposition (together with Parliament as the seat of sovereignty and the multi-party system).

The socialist states are an important sub-group in the category of states whose political systems do not comprise the institution of political opposition. Most of these have parliaments supreme soviets, national assemblies), and in some of them several political parties or groups survive (Poland, the G.D.R., Czechoslovakia, China). In the U.S.S.R. non-party candidates, and in Yugoslavia and Hungary a proportion of multi-candidates, are allowed in some constituencies. Yet, in spite of all this, the general and principal rule is that the other parties or non-party candidates, or any organisation in the state, are forbidden to compete for power with the 'single' or 'hegemonic' communist (or workers') party.

The ideological reason for this distinctive political feature is that as the socialist states are on their way towards classless, conflictless socialist forms, open competition for power by several political parties must be seen as a relic of the past: when there were classes in the society, when there were conflicts between them, and when the political parties were the political articulation of these conflicts. In a society which is building socialism these relics of the past must be banned. (Lenin explicitly banned opposition at the Tenth Congress, in 1921.)

B. THE COMPARATIVE STUDY OF THE SOCIALIST STATE AS A TRANSITIONAL FORM AND AS AN IDEOLOGICAL ANOMALY

The second reason why the study of the socialist state is recommended as a peg for comparative communist political studies is that the continuing existence of the state after the revolution is, in pure logic, a contradiction *in adjecto*. Lenin's exclamation in 1916: 'But further on Marx speaks of "the future state of communist society" ! ! Thus even in *communist* society the state will exist! Is there not a contradiction in this?' express in all sincerity the fundamental dilemma of the post-revolutionary political organisation. For the student of comparative communist *politics* there can be no better vantage-point from which to observe (a) the essential difference between socialist theory and praxis; (b) the permanent contradiction and ill-adjustments *in* and *between* the institutions of socialist politics: i.e. those deriving from the socialist idea of decentralised direct and self-administration, and those superimposed by the growth of the arch-centralistic 'total' state; and (c) the deep ideological differences between the schools of thought clashing in the communist world movement and notably the Russian, the Chinese and the Yugoslav.

As has been noted,[57] the decision on what form to adopt for the post-revolutionary political organisation (whether it should be yet another form of nation-state, i.e. with a population contained within a territory submitted to the sovereignty of one central government, or whether it should be a communist form of federation of mutualistic communes and corporations) was only taken almost a year after the Bolshevik Revolution of 1917, and by a Constituent Commission fundamentally divided on this issue.

This division remains at the heart of opposition from within the communist movement against 'bureaucracy'. It is, now, characteristic not only of the contemporary ideological fight between the New Left (anarcho-syndicalist, Trotskyist or anarchist) and the established communist parties, but also at a much deeper level, and with much more direct implications on the actual political structures of the triangular polemic, between the three major schools of Marxist-Leninist political thought. Lenin's contribution to the *political* part of Marxist-Leninist theory is far more important than Marx's.[58] But, whereas Lenin's contribution to the *pre-revolutionary* and *revolutionary* political theory is uniquely important, his views on *post-revolutionary* political organisation remained, on paper, as contradictory as anything that Marx and Engels wrote on the subject. His admirable tightrope exercise on the notion of a commune-state (the present 'soviet-state') has proved its precariousness: the 'state' has absorbed the 'soviets' and his theory (based on crumbs from Marx and Engels) of the *transitional* 'state of the dictatorship of the proletariat' has been proved false by the fact that the state has remained permanent, and indeed has grown from strength to strength. In addition, this theory is now fragmented among the successional schools of Marxist-Leninist political thought.

Currently the doctrine of the C.P.S.U., which has to defend the existence of the formidable state of the U.S.S.R., this arch-centralistic state-organisation, stands on the definitional position taken at the Twenty-Second Congress, namely that the dictatorship of the proletariat has of late been superseded by the 'state of the whole people'. (But see, for a more detailed and up-to-date view on this question, Roger E. Kanet, 'The Rise and Fall of the "All-People's State" ' in *Soviet Studies,* xx 1, July 1968.) This new state remains necessary as long as the 'social organisations' have not acquired sufficient strength to produce their own means of self-administration, and to replace the central controls. At this stage the party also remains necessary, and its role is seen by the new statutes to be 'enhanced' in this new phase. The difference between the state of the dictatorship of the proletariat and the state of the whole people amounts, therefore, in political terms to very little. The differences, for example in the operation known as de-Stalinsation, are made to bear merely on the style of leadership, and the legality and flexibility of the administrative process.

The contemporary Soviet doctrine is criticised by the Chinese-Maoist political theory which attacks in particular the inconsistency, in Marxist-Leninist logic, of pretending that the dictatorship of the proletariat can be dispensed with as long as the classes, and the inevitable 'contradictions' between them, subsist. But, this being said, it must not be forgotten that Chinese political theory was from the beginning much more anti-bureaucratic, anti-state and anti-institutional than the Soviet doctrine. Although the present state is seen as a centralised structure needed for the period of the 'democratic dictatorship' led by the working class, the accent is laid on the autonomy of the local organisation : 'autonomous *chou,* counties and cities'. Organs of self-government are established in all these administrative divisions. But whereas the letter of the constitution is not very different from that of the Soviet constitution (and is in many respects sharper in its definitions of the 'transitional' political institutions), the ideological Maoist orientation is anti-bureaucratic. Bureaucracy is seen as the grave-digger of the revolution, which if it is to remain alive requires permanent rejuvenation and integration with the masses by means of cultural revolution. The party itself is seen only as the third element in the trinity party–army–cultural revolution which is at the basis of the revolutionary committees, the agencies of this unarrested revolution.

The Yugoslav doctrine differs from both the Soviet and the Chinese. Yugoslav political theory is based on the assumption that Yugoslav society can already dispense with the structures of central state-controls, and has entered the superior stage of self-management and decentralisation which alone, in its eyes, can be considered as socialist. The Yugoslav doctrine denounces the 'dictatorship of the proletariat' as a cover for the Stalinist forms of bureaucracy which lead, functionally and inevitably, to the monstrous aberrations of totalitarianism. In the Yugoslav doctrine the state and central bureaucracy have already started to wither away and power has already been diffused in the entire society or community. The party itself, now known as the League of Communists, is seen as abdicating its right of control and direct guidance, and being absorbed into increasingly broader deliberative bodies, until it finally merges with the self-administered society.

It is understandable that from a comparative point of view the study of the theory and praxis of these three Marxist-Leninist interpretations of the problem of political organisation, as well as of all the nuances on the spectrum of this problem represented by the theories of the other Marxist-Leninist parties, is the most rewarding.

It might also be said that the different political processes thus engendered by the different Marxist-Leninist political theories, oscillating as they do inconclusively between the decentralised 'commune' and the centralistic 'state', can be equated with the antagonistic processes of political mobilisation and of political participation.[59] But as soon as we say this, we have to ask whether these two alternatives are not also and primarily two stages of political processes in the evolution of the economy of societies from pre-industrial to industrialised and post-industrial.

C. THE COMPARATIVE STUDY OF THE SOCIALIST STATE IN THE INDUSTRIAL-TECHNOLOGICAL AGE

Yet another reason why the comparative examination of the socialist states *qua* states is justified is that like all other nation-states in this technological age they are faced with acute problems of modernisation, indeed of survival. So profound were and are the changes in the economic and social processes, and institutions, of the contemporary industrial-technological society, that the modernisation of the old political processes and institutions is imminently required. Sovereignty and its embodiment, the nation-state, are directly challenged. The classic notion of the sovereignty of the nation-state is yielding to the active processes of *internationalisation*, and its corollary, *integration* in larger inter- or supra-national units. It is exploded from within by the new forms of representation (the group, or 'functional' entity, and the regional, or sectional, representations, showing a greater effective- ness than the political, or national, forms of representation) and by the new processes of participation : participation by self-man- agement and by communication. This other approach to the comparative examination of the socialist state is also *critical*, in the sense that it is best undertaken in the light of its *crisis*. Whereas in the previous section what was proposed for comparative exam- ination was the crisis of the socialist state as an ideological contra- diction, as the state which should never have been a state, what is recommended here is the comparative examination of the socialist state as the nation-state in quest of survival, as an old institution which might have to be replaced by other institutions, or which in any case will have to undergo profound transformations.

This comparative examination could be undertaken on both planes : intra-area and cross-area. To be sure, the changes pro- duced in modern societies by the technological age affect all states and their political processes. But in so far as the socialist states are the most centralistic states, these changes affect them most especially. Each of these aspects deserves to be studied separately.

(a) Intra-area

The socialist state is the most centralistic of all modern states. Yet the need for *decentralisation* of the Leninist-Stalinist administra- tive machine is obvious. It is no longer capable of coping with the tasks of control and supervision required by the interdependent industrial society. These obligations are both too numerous and too technically specialised for any administrative machine, let alone this particularly inflexible one.

The first and major change in the running of the centralised socialist states occurred when most of them reached the first stage of industrialisation. By now, from the point of view of economic development, the socialist states can be divided into : highly indus- trialised (technological) – the U.S.S.R., the G.D.R., and Czecho- slovakia; industrialised – Hungary, Yugoslavia, and Poland;

undergoing intensive industrialisation – Romania, China and Bulgaria; still to be industrialised – Albania, Cuba, North Vietnam, North Korea and Outer Mongolia.

These degrees of industrial development are reflected in differences in the political processes which can broadly be described as those between *mobilisation* and *participation*. This means that the political process of mobilisation (taken in a narrow literal sense), i.e. the concentration, under one unique centre of command, of all resources of capital, manpower and raw materials for one global economic operation, politically suits the need fo. centralisation required by the first stages of industrialisation (the take-off) or more precisely the period required by the First Economic Plans in any state undergoing industrialisation. It is also presumed that the *total* control thus assumed by the state over the totality of the society following such a national plan of growth, amounts to excessively centralised (even totalitarian) forms of political rule. In contradistinction to this it is also assumed that once the first level of industrialisation is reached, and the national industrial structure with its hard core of heavy industry has been erected, its functioning cannot be served any longer by the political processes of command and implementation. What is operative in the new forms of production and in the new services is *efficiency*.

But the greater the need for efficiency, the greater also the need for voluntary participation of those employed. And the more complex and interdependent the entire process of the running of the economy, the stronger the bargaining-power of the innumerable groups engaged in these processes. By the sheer threat of ceasing their participation they can paralyse the functioning of the economy.

If this was as straightforward as it sounds, the result of this reasoning should be a clear table in which the most advanced industrial, technological socialist states would show the highest indices of decentralisation, devolution of power, new representations and adoption of participatory techniques and processes. This is contradicted by the fact that, for instance, the U.S.S.R. and the G.D.R., the two most industrialised socialist states, are also the most centralistic; but it is confirmed by the fact that of all communist parties the Czechoslovak party, which rules one of the most developed and technologically advanced socialist states, was able to propose the most coherent and articulated economic, social, and political reforms of all the socialist states. It is clear that in assessing the evolution from mobilisation to participation many other factors must be taken into consideration. These are, for instance : the degree of autonomy of the different socialist states (see in the next subsection: *cross-area*); the differences between the immense strength and intact sovereignty of the super-power and the 'penetrated' sovereignty of the other nation-states; the level of political and economic development, and of 'political culture' (in which, of course, the history of the state concerned and of its peoples plays a prominent part); the degree of decentralisation already obtained in each of the socialist states by way of self-management and direct administration or by way of decentralisation for industrial-technological reasons; the degree of participation obtained in individual socialist states for reasons other than socio-economic (as, for instance, the amount of popular backing obtained for nationalistic reasons by different communist parties when resisting some external pressures, either from non-socialist states or indeed from communist states : the U.S.S.R. in most cases, but Yugoslavia in the case of Albania, Bulgaria in the case of Yugoslavia, etc.), as well as many other factors.

But generally speaking, the change from the political process of excessively centralised mobilisation to the political processes of gradually decentralising participation can be best absorbed from angles like the following : the changing role of the state (this should be considered mainly under the heading of cross-area study); the economic reforms (the examination of the kind of economic reforms undertaken by individual socialist states, as well as the effects their implementation produces on the social and political institutions); the changing role of the party (attitudes across the spectrum from the U.S.S.R. to China and Yugoslavia, and from, for instance, the self-assertive parties of Romania, Bulgaria and the G.D.R. to the self-effacing party of Hungary); the changing role of the judiciary (the degree of autonomy granted to the judiciary, from the new 'socialist legality' observed after 'de-Stalinisation' in the U.S.S.R., to the establishment of the Constitutional Court in Yugoslavia); the changing relations between the legislature and the executives (the extent of differences which can be observed between the electoral laws and the parliamentary procedures in the Soviet Union and Romania, or Yugoslavia, Poland, and Hungary – and at different periods in each of these states); the growth of group-representation (the greater or lesser degree of influence and bargaining-power in the processes of decision-making of the technical intelligentsia, the trade unions, the workers' councils and all other 'groups' form a highly relevant comparative spectrum); the changing role of communication – the extent of the usefulness or the counter-productiveness in the individual socialist states of the ideologically centralised means of communication can be measured in relation to the amount of independent information demanded and absorbed, i.e. from foreign sources (press, radio, and, in the case of Czechoslovakia, the G.D.R. and Hungary, even television) but also and especially in relation to the indigenous or underground counter-cultures (the non-official or clandestine fringe publications and circles); the articulation of political opposition (studies of the politicisation of the 'groups', of the emergence of 'parliamentary groups', and of factions in the party, should be added, when and if they can be undertaken).

(b) Cross-area

Most of the effects of the transformation of the socialist state caused by the transition from pre-industrial to technological societies are similar to the effects the same causes produce on non-socialist states. To be sure, one cannot ignore the fact that most of the pluralistic-constitutional states of the West have gone through their primary industrialisation long before the U.S.S.R. and East European countries. The anachronism is less blatant in the last period when the U.S.S.R., having completed the first industrialisation under Stalin, proceeded at once to catch up with the West, and especially with the U.S.A., during the transition towards the high technological stages. But one cannot ignore the fact that the political institutions and processes are so thoroughly different that the political effects of similar economic and social changes in the two types of state are comparable only within the respective backgrounds. Nothing in the evolution observed since they entered the rapid changes of the technological age proves that both groups will give similar political answers to the similar economic socio-questions of the day. It might well happen that in the new circumstances they will drift further apart.

But most of the causes are indeed comparable. The groups in both kinds of societies are stimulated by the processes of modern industrial production into demanding new participatory rights in the major processes of decision-making. Group representation becomes one of the commanding features of both societies – in one eclipsing to a certain degree the supremacy of political representation, in the other introducing a new element of representation and reducing the previously unchallenged rights of the political leaderships to take all decisions with a minimum of consultation of the representative groups in the society. The growing accumulation and specialisation of problems to be solved by the central organs opens in both societies a yawning gap between the politician (or the Red) and the expert; and, in both groups of societies, the demand for decentralisation (in the sense of transfer of power to the regions), and devolution (in the sense of transfer of power to the corporate basis of the society), becomes more pressing. In both groups of societies the intensification of communication through the new mass media, and through the expansion of literacy, should be able to produce an intensification of participation in the general political discussion and bring all major issues 'into the street'. In both groups of societies the cleavage between generations becomes more accentuated as the rapid technological changes transform not only the human *mores* but even human psychology and human nature. These new socioeconomic phenomena, with similar aspects regardless of the political régimes in which they occur, can sometimes even produce apparently similar crises, as was the case of the simultaneous events in the spring of 1968 in two almost neighbouring states, the one socialist, Czechoslovakia, and the other pluralistic-constitutional, France. It is here that the efforts of comparative examination made by sociology and political sociology are so important. It is in these more abstract and much more highly conceptualised fields that the comparative analysis could cut across the institutional barriers.

Socialist and non-socialist states engaged in the technological evolution are commonly faced with the two-pronged alternatives of: (*a*) diffusion of responsibilities in the processes of decision-making within their own national communities in quest of participation, and yet (*b*) integration and super-coordination in new centres, larger territorial units rendered necessary by the internationalisation of the economy and of communications as well as by the new centralisation required by the very technology. This leads directly to the problem of sovereignty in either of its Janus-faces. Under (*a*) the internal sovereignty of the central government is fragmented in the new multiplicity of centres of decision-making emerging through the new political and social processes. Under (*b*) the external sovereignty is seen under pressure from without, from the stronger forces at large in the international world, which act together above the previously effective boundaries of the nation-states. This seems to call for larger, integrated communities which, by the fusion and amalgamation of the faltering individual states, would produce quasi-federal sovereignties capable of resisting the pressures of the international forces, markets and organisations.

REFERENCES

1. *Government and Opposition*, v 1 (winter 1969–70).
2. *American Political Science Review*, no. 4 (Dec 1970).
3. D. Richard Little, 'Communist Studies in a Comparative Framework', p. 94, in Fleron, op. cit. (Chicago : Rand McNally, 1969).
4. In the introduction to vol. i of *A History of Soviet Russia* (London : Macmillan, 1950).
5. Isaac Deutscher, 'The Roots of Bureaucracy', in *The Socialist Register, 1969* (London : The Merlin Press, 1969).
6. Ibid., p. 28.
7. *The Open Society and its Enemies* (London : Kegan Paul, 1945).
8. *The Origins of Totalitarianism* (New York : Harcourt, Brace, 1957).
9. *The Origins of Totalitarian Democracy* (London : Secker & Warburg, 1961).
10. Harvard U. P., 1956.
11. *How Russia is Ruled* (Harvard U.P., 1963). Thus : 'The ruling party is self-perpetuating and it cannot be dislodged save by revolution. Its powers are all-embracing and without limit. So-called "constitutional" arrangements derive such force as they possess from the régime's sanction' (pp. 349–50).
12. 'I have borrowed the term "apparat" from G. Ionescu's *The Politics of the European Communist States* (London : Weidenfeld & Nicolson, 1967). But, as is evident, I cannot accept his terminology "apparat state" : the apparat, in my interpretation, is not one *kind* of state, but something different from, and inimical to, the state' (from 'The Concept of Totalitarianism', *Survey*, autumn 1969, p. 103).
13. 'Soviet and Communist Politics : A Comparative Approach', *Journal of Politics*, xxii (May 1960).
14. 'On the Comparative Study of Communism', *World Politics*, xix 2 (Jan 1967).

15. 'Comparing Communist Nations : Prospects for an Empirical Approach', *American Political Science Review*, no. 1 (Mar 1968).

16. 'Soviet Area Studies and the Social Sciences : Some Methodological Problems in Communist Studies', *Soviet Studies*, xix 3 (Jan 1968).

17. The organisers of the very useful conference on 'Political Leadership in Eastern Europe and the Soviet Union' held in November 1968 under the auspices of the Comparative Politics Program at Northwestern University. Published under this title by Aldine, Chicago, 1970.

18. The organiser of the conference on 'Change in Communist Systems' held at Berkeley under the auspices of the A.C.L.S. Planning Committee for Comparative Communist Studies, and published under this title by Stanford University Press, 1970.

19. *The Politics of the European Communist States*, and as the organiser of the study in comparative politics sponsored by the Social Science Research Council, and at present carried out by eight British universities, on 'The Social and Political Processes in Eastern Europe' (1968–71).

20. 'The Comparative Study of Communist Political Systems', *Slavic Review*, xxvi (Mar 1967).

21. Op. cit., p. 1044. See above, p. 8.

22. See Paul Shoup and David E. Powell, 'The Emergence of Political Science in Communist Countries', *American Political Science Review*, no. 2 (June 1970).

23. Columbus, Ohio : Charles E. Merrill Publishing Co., 1969.

24. Boston and Toronto : Little, Brown, 1966. Barghoorn was also one of the first sovietologists who agreed to submit his studies to the team-treatment of one common conceptual umbrella and contributed the article on 'Soviet Russia : Orthodoxy and Adaptiveness' to Lucian Pye and Sidney Verba's *Political Culture and Political Development* (Princeton U.P., 1965).

25. Princeton U.P., 1968.

26. London : Weidenfeld & Nicolson, 1970.

27. Reproduced in Fleron, *Communist Studies and the Social Sciences*.

28. 'As political scientists have become increasingly concerned with the adaptation and transformation of political systems, and particularly with problems of public policy relating to the new nations, there has been an increasing tendency to focus on the interaction of whole political systems with their domestic and

international environments, since it is at this level that it becomes possible to explain political change. This most recent development among students of comparative politics and political development holds out the prospect of bridging the discontinuity between empirical and normative political theories' (in the article 'Comparative Politics' in *International Encyclopaedia of the Social Sciences* (New York : Macmillan, 1968) xii 334).

29. *Society, Culture and Personality, their Structure and Dynamics: A System of General Sociology* (New York : Cooper, 1947).

30. New York : John Day, 1941.

31. Oxford : Clarendon Press, 1953.

32. New York : Norton, 1953.

33. In his preface to *18 Lectures on Industrial Society* (London : Weidenfeld & Nicolson, 1961).

34. London : Chatto & Windus, 1964.

35. See especially S. A. Khavina. *A Critique of Bourgeois Views on the Laws of Socialist Economic Management* (Moscow, 1968).

36. In his *The Process of Government,* ed. Peter H. Odegard (Harvard U.P., 1967; first published 1907).

37. Especially *Studies in the Problem of Sovereignty* (New Haven : Yale U.P., 1918).

38. New York : Knopf, 1957.

39. 'Group Conflict and Political Change', in Chalmers Johnson, op. cit., pp. 221–2.

40. *World Politics,* xvi (July 1964).

41. In a particularly substantial and original essay on 'The Rationalisation of Party Control', in Chalmers Johnson, op. cit., p. 153.

42. *Slavic Review* (Mar 1967).

43. In Chalmers Johnson, op. cit., pp. 375–6.

44. For instance, the somewhat impressionistic but pioneering works of Hugh Seton-Watson. His *The East European Revolution* (London : Methuen, 1950) remains one of the first works to have singled out with authority the importance of the study of the intelligentsia in that 'revolution' and in its subsequent phase of consolidation. It still maintains a distinct usefulness owing to its blending of the historical facts with a rewarding inclination to suggest general, comparative conclusions.

45. For a proper discussion of the importance of the concept of the state in contemporary political science, or indeed of 'political science as statecraft', see, in this series of Studies in Comparative

Politics, W. J. M. Mackenzie, *The Study of Political Science Today*, and especially the section on 'Statecraft, and Politics without States' (pp. 15–18).

46. For instance to Almond and Powell's bold exclamation : 'The older texts used such terms as "government", "nation" or "state" to describe what we call a political system. Something more is involved here than mere style of nomenclature. This new terminology reflects a new way of looking at political phenomena' (*Comparative Politics: A Developmental Approach*, p. 16). S. E. Finer answers by showing that the same authors are afterwards using the concept of state with different names and sometimes even with its own name, as in 'state building' (in *Government and Opposition*, v 1, pp. 3–21). And Jean Blondel in his *Introduction to Comparative Government* (London : Weidenfeld & Nicolson, 1969) : 'We are left with only one approach to the study of government : it consists of studying national governments across national boundaries.'

47. Chalmers Johnson, op. cit., pp. i–xxxii.

48. In Fleron, op. cit., p. 190.

49. Article 2 of the 1936 U.S.S.R. Constitution : 'The political foundation of the U.S.S.R. is the Soviets of Toilers' Deputies'; and Article 3 : 'all power in the U.S.S.R. belongs to the toilers of town and country as represented by the Soviets of Toilers' Deputies'. Article 2 of the 1954 Chinese Constitution : 'All power in the People's Republic of China belongs to the people. The organs through which the people exercise power are the National People's Congress and the local people's congresses at various levels'; and Article 23 : 'The National People's Congress is composed of deputies elected by provinces' . . . etc. Article 2 of the 1949 Hungarian Constitution : 'In the Hungarian People's Republic all power belongs to the working class. The workers of town and country exercise their power through their elected representatives, who are responsible and accountable to the people'. And even in the more modern and sophisticated 1963 Yugoslav Constitution, Article 74 : 'The functions of power and government of social affairs shall be exercised by representative bodies.' As far as the practicality of representativeness is concerned even the first (1918) Russian Constitution solved in an arithmetical way the problem by stating that in the All-Russian Congress of Soviets there would be one delegate of the

urban soviets for 25,000 voters, and one for 125,000 voters of the *guberniya* soviets. On this question see also Otto Bihari, *Socialist Representative Institutions* (Budapest, 1970).

50. Article 5, 1936 Constitution.
51. In the 'Basic Principles' of the 1963 Constitution.
52. Articles 5–7, 1954 Constitution.
53. The expression was used in this sense by the author of this survey in his *The Politics of the European Communist States.*
54. In the 25-point letter of the C.C.P. of 14 June 1963.
55. In *The Politics of the European Communist States,* and in G. Ionescu and Isabel de Madariaga, *Opposition* (London : C. A. Watts, 1968).
56. Expression coined by Raymond Aron in *Democracy and Totalitarianism* (London : Weidenfeld & Nicolson, 1968).
57. See also 'Lenin, the Commune and the State', by this author in *Government and Opposition,* v 2 (spring 1970).
58. 'What is to supersede the smashed state-machine? In 1848, in the *Communist Manifesto,* Marx's answer to this question was still a purely abstract one, or, to speak more correctly, it was an answer that indicated the problem but did not solve it' (*State and Revolution,* 1917).
59. 'So conceived, participation is the very opposite, or the very reverse of mobilisation. Mobilisation does not convey the idea of individual self-motion, but the idea of a malleable, passive collectivity which is being *put into motion* at the whim of persuasive – and more than persuasive – authorities. We say that individuals "participate", but we cannot say about the same individuals that they "mobilise" – they are *mobilised* !' (Giovanni Sartori, 'Concept Misformation in Comparative Politics', *American Political Science Review,* LXIV 4 (Dec 1970) 1050–1).